Negative of a Group Photograph

نگاتیو یک عکس دسته جمعی

NEGATIVE OF A GROUP PHOTOGRAPH
نگاتیو یک عکس دسته جمعی

Azita Ghahreman
آزیتا قهرمان

Translated by Maura Dooley

with Elhum Shakerifar

BLOODAXE BOOKS

Poems © Azita Ghahreman 2018
Translations © Maura Dooley 2018
Introduction © Elhum Shakerifar 2018

ISBN: 978 1 78037 436 9

First published in 2018 by
Bloodaxe Books Ltd
Eastburn
South Park
Hexham
Northumberland NE46 1BS

in association with
The Poetry Translation Centre Ltd
The Albany, Douglas Way
London SE8 4AG

www.bloodaxebooks.com
www.poetrytranslation.org

This book has been selected to receive financial assistance from English PEN's
PEN Translates programme, supported by Arts Council England. English PEN
exists to promote literature and our understanding of it, to uphold writers'
freedoms around the world, to campaign against the persecution and impris-
onment of writers for stating their views, and to promote the friendly co-
operation of writers and the free exchange of ideas.
www.englishpen.org

Designed in Albertina by Aftab Publication
Cover photograph from the author's personal collection
Cover design by North Kuras, Exploded View
Printed in the UK by Bell & Bain Ltd, Glasgow, Scotland on acid-free paper
sourced from mills with FSC chain of custody certification.

Contents

Remembering with affection and gratitude
Sarah Maguire,
poet, translator and founding director of
the Poetry Translation Centre.
Her warmth, hard work and vision brought together
poets from all over the world.

Introduction

Azita Ghahreman was born in Mashhad in 1962 and has lived and worked in Sweden since 2006. Her poetry has been translated into many languages including Swedish, German, Dutch and French; this book brings together the most comprehensive English language translation of her work to date. In selecting poems from across Azita's entire oeuvre, we wanted to reflect the diversity of styles and themes in her work. The poems selected here span almost four decades, representing work throughout Azita's career from the earliest of her five published books to several poems published for the first time.

Much of Azita's work is deeply personal yet infused with political undertones. Her poems often reflect on her childhood growing up in a land-owning family in the South-Eastern Khorasan province of Iran – referenced in evocative images of the natural world amongst which she grew up – and on the changing face of modern Iran. In the poem 'Glaucoma', taken from her third collection of poetry, *Forgetfulness is a Simple Ritual* (1992), the changes to Iran's political landscape are referenced as gradual blindness that slowly blurs the vision. Azita depicts her own family who, despite their differing affiliations and beliefs, still remain deeply connected, in the same way that Iran – a country that is home to numerous ethnicities and belief systems – continues to retain its united entity.

Thinkers and political leaders are often referenced by name: the philosopher, Nietzsche; the physicist, Oppenheimer; the poet, Nima Youshij (referred to in Persian by his first name only, a familiarity that is common with many of the country's independence leaders of the 1960s, all find their way into Azita's work. The censored and unspoken are also present: in 'When Winter Comes', the narrator warms herself at the fire created by her own burning books. 'With a Red Flower', taken from the collection *Sculptures of Autumn* (1986), is dedicated to a lost friend whose name can only be read between the lines of a poem; much like the poppies one wears to remember veterans in the UK, the red flower in Iran represents political prisoners. Azita's early work carries many references to the political repression as well as to the images of Iraq's destroyed streets – images that were televised regularly during the Iran-Iraq War, which lasted almost a decade.

Azita's third collection *The Suburb of Crows* (2008) reflects on her migration to Sweden. 'The Boat That Brought Me' tells of the burdens of exile, the loss of one's homeland and of her first impressions of this new country:

> Sometimes I miss
> the boat that brought me here,
> now that I am witness to the icy eyes of a Swedish winter
> under these tired old clouds,
> while that suitcase still holds a patch of the sky-blue me.

The lonely stranger-crow, its dark plumage contrasting against the falling snow, is a recurring symbol of Sweden. Yet 'When Winter Comes' sees the years in exile pass quickly and quietly, 'galloping by like a wild, dark horse'.

A constant and most refreshing theme throughout Azita's work is her unusual approach to the classic theme of love. When it comes to love, the poet's grave and solemn voice becomes playful. In 'The First Rains of Spring', we are advised that it is best to 'keep love at bay'; for in the end:

... what have we gained from it?
Only the last winds of autumn,
the first rains of spring.

In the poem 'Happy Valentine', the poet becomes wicked and taunting as she enumerates the calamities she will bring upon her lover.

I'll pop a cockroach in your drink and a drawing pin
  in your shoe,
move all the pieces on the board and ruin every game

Womanhood is also a strong theme – Azita's is an undeniably feminine voice, her world feels distinctly matriarchal and references to her grandmother, mother and daughter find their way into many of her poems – often as protectors. In 'Spring', a poem that sees no joy accompany the first days of the new season (Iranian New Year, known as 'Naw Ruz' – literally 'new day' – is celebrated on the Spring equinox every year), it is striking that Spring is a woman and that she is undeterred by the horrors of the Iran-Iraq war that have ravaged the country over the course of the year:

she always comes back
sometimes with death at her breast,
skirts singed by war,
face stained with mud

Circling back every year, Spring in this poem embodies the constant, reassuring presence of women in Azita's work. Her arrival marks renewal, growth, life. She is here to unstitch and re-stitch clothes, for children who have grown a little taller over the course of the year. She recognises and acknowledges pain and grief, and with her needle and thread, gives it an outlet:

> sewing, in every nook and cranny, in cerulean thread,
> the image of a bird –
>
> pain like a green stone, in place of its eyes
> and a wound where its beak should be,
> so it can sing out   its scarlet song.

Poetry itself is a recurring theme – often a trustworthy companion in a confused world – 'the only fresh clothes that I knew' – as well as a reason to keep going during darker days of political unrest:

> I am alive
> in poems yet to be sung,
> in fragments of myself, scattered to the wind.

In the early days of exile, Azita mourns the absence of her beloved Farsi, and reflects on the confusion of a new language:

> I am not stripped of word and thought
> but sometimes what I want to say gets lost

However, words trace a path forwards – the poet can belong anywhere:

> but poetry is headstrong, walks barefoot,
> cannot be directed, has no true home

In 2012, Azita, Maura and I were brought together by the Poetry Translation Centre to translate a small selection of Azita's poetry into English. Working together for the second time, and on a significantly more ambitious endeavour, I have reflected often over the last 18 months on the process of being a bridge between two poets, two languages, two worlds. The Persian language is expressive, sometimes overwhelmingly so, prone to extremes of emotion, words often loaded with meaning. On the other hand, the English language tends to be descriptive, informative. It is a language of exactitude, whilst Persian is surely a language of in-between. Yet to convey a sense of ambivalence in an English translation could be misread, or confuse – might bring into question the translation, rather than to indicate the vastness of variables in the original. There is no easy transition from one to the other. As a 'bridge translator', I built the 'slippery, twisty bridge' that Azita writes about in her poem 'Words' – a poem that begins with a woman in one guise, who 'hides herself behind words / so that you have to search for her' but who reappears by the end of the poem as an unrecognisable iteration of herself.

The journey from one language to the other is well illustrated in 'In the Depths of Time', a poem in which endless rain has pooled between the days – 'words burst like silver bubbles' and 'love had been washed away'. As the poet recalls these days, the picture of a woman comes to mind. My literal translation of this verse reads as follows:

> I no longer remember
> Apart from a misty road
> And the repeated passage of a woman with an angular body
> Whose invisible ropes have passed the bony ladders of
>   despair

This was accompanied by several notes, expanding on the meanings of certain words, for example that the word used to define this woman in Persian references outlines, angles, nets, squares. I noted that my use of the word 'angular' was almost an interpretation, and that it could be understood literally as 'netted', or even 'possible to see through'. I also noted that that passage is implied in both movement and time.

In the literal translations, I would offer several options of how to understand key words and where the images were complex, Maura and I would talk about meaning, interpretation, Maura's questions would dig deeper into meaning, understanding the context, painting a fuller picture – why is she angular? What do the ladders of despair represent? Azita explained this as a dark image, of a woman who is somehow angular, in pieces, through which we can see the bonds that hold her back.

This literal translation is a good example of its own role as stepping stone. The ideas in these lines sit uneasily in the English language – the words don't chime, it doesn't feel logical, it is at risk of being too confused to make sense of. Maura's poetry, however, is none of these things. It reframes (from 'not remembering' to 'all that comes' to memory) and in doing so finds a way to remain distinctly close to the original description – in essence, in words and in meaning:

> Now, all that comes to me
> is a misty road
> and the endless journeying of a woman
> whose jagged body
> was held back
> by invisible ties,
> a rope ladder of despair.

There are many more examples to choose from. I often marvelled at the simplicity of touch that Maura brought to sentences that by the nature of translation became convoluted in English. The first lines of 'Every Tangled Branch' are a beautiful example of this. The literal translation was an unwieldy couplet that read:

> Like the disheveled look of the locust-tree with its hanging
>   clusters
> Chandeliers of white ringlets trembling in the wind

This was accompanied by a note that the word for ringlets is more commonly the word hyacinth. It was transformed into the following lines – closer to the Persian both in musicality and imagery, and therefore elegance:

> The locust-tree looked ruffled,
> its hanging clusters
> like chandeliers of white ringlets trembling in the breeze.

The years separating the first set of translations and the latest selection have played an important part – allowing Azita, Maura and me to come to know each other as people as well as wordsmiths. It has been a humbling process to reflect on the words of a living poet – Azita generously took the time to unpack images, explain the worlds she had hidden behind words, unravel inferred expressions and stories, as well as to embrace departures from words as symbols in order to better convey meaning or emotion. On the other side of the bridge, with vast patience and attention to detail, Maura absorbed volumes of stories and deftly balanced the exactitude of English words with the meanings in between. It should also be noted that the fine alchemy of Azita and Maura's poetic voices is a legacy of the late poet and founder of the Poetry Translation Centre, Sarah Maguire.

Azita's poetry is complex: individual words can have

multiple meanings and paradoxes can inflect the logic in her poems. Her voice can vary wildly from one poem to the next – from amorous expression to sharp witticism, from solemn to playful. In these translations we have tried to remain loyal to the rich imagery of Persian poetry, as well as help an English-speaking audience grasp the layers of meaning behind Azita's words.

Elhum Shakerifar

Negative of a Group Photograph

نگاتیو یک عکس دسته جمعی

دوچرخه قرمز

هنوز خواب می‌بینم
دوچرخه قرمزم را
بر ساحل سبز تابستان
سایه موهایم پریشان در آب
مشق‌هایم پر از حبه‌های انگور

بزرگ شدن قد کشیدنی دشوار بود
در هوای خار و سنگ
از کف دادن ِ یک‌یک تیله‌های رنگارنگ

بی همبازی کنار کوچه نشستن
با دوچرخه‌ی زنگ‌زده‌ای در انبار
عکسی از جاده‌ای سبز بر دیوار

Red Bicycle

I still dream
of my red bicycle
on the green shores of summer,
my unruly hair casting shadows on the water,
my school work peppered with grape pips.

Pulling away, growing up, was hard
in that weather of thorns and stones,
I let the bright shining marbles slip from my fingers, one by one.

No-one to play with, I sat by the side of the road,
my bicycle, rusty in the shed,
that green shore, a picture on the wall.

دیو شب

شب از کوچه‌ای نزدیک
با بوی کتاب‌های سوخته
می‌آید و سر می‌گذارد بر شیشه اتاق
به دست‌های مادربزرگ می‌پیچد
به چرخش کند دانه‌های تسبیح
بر چین‌های دامن سیاهش
به گهواره کودک خیره می‌شود
با جیب‌های خالی از ماه و ستاره
با پیشانی زخمی
تا کنار داوودی‌های سپید و ساعت دیواری
تا بشقاب‌های خالی
و قصه‌های مادربزرگ آمده است
با دهانی از دود و خاکستر

Night Demon

At night, from the nearby street

the stink of burning books

presses in through the window,

finds the pleats of Grandmother's dark skirt,

twists round her hands

as she slowly turns her prayer beads.

It stares at the baby's cradle.

Pockets emptied out of moon and stars,

battle-scarred,

it has crept all the way up to

the white chrysanthemums, the clock on the wall,

to our empty plates,

all the way up to Grandmother's stories –

a mouth of smoke and ashes.

گمشده

تقدیم به خاطره مادربزرگ

از خواب‌ها که پیاده می‌شدیم
صبح روشن بود
روزِ گرسنه، گربه‌وار می‌چرخید
به دور پاهایش

عطر جوشانده‌ها و خش‌خشِ جارو
نورهای شادمان سر می‌رفت
از قابِ کهنه‌ی چوبی

ماجرا از فرط سادگی کمی سخت است
چیزی نبرده لخت رفته است
با انگشت‌ها، با صورت و صدایش
بی‌اجازه، عین دختربچه‌ای پابرهنه و سرخود

ردش تا همین‌جاست
دیگ خالی، شمعدانی‌های خشک
و تسبیحِ سیاه لای کتاب
بعد بادها می‌چرخند
و برگ‌ها می‌ریزند
روی صفحه‌ای که از سنگ است
و دیگر ورق نمی‌خورد

The Lost

In memory of my Grandmother

We stepped out of sleep
into a brilliant morning.
The day hungry, the way a cat
might weave around your legs

and in the scent of simmering remedies and the swish-swish of the
   broom
our bright happiness overflowed
its frame of memories.

What happened next is difficult; death is such an everyday event.
She took nothing, and left, as she came, naked,
with just her hands, her face, her voice,
without permission, like a stubborn, barefoot little girl.
Traces of her still persist
in an empty pot, in dried flowers,
in her black prayer beads threaded through the pages of a book.
The winds sweep and swirl
and leaves scatter
across a page of stone
that now can no longer be turned.

آب سیاه

شقایق‌ها اول آمدند
ملخ‌ها بعد وقت باد
این تمام کودکی چشم‌های تو بود
پیش از آب سیاه و تیغ
رشته‌های هزار مسجد
از گل‌های دیوانه رد می‌شد

اول شقایق‌ها رفته‌اند
بعد مادربزرگ و اتاق نمور شازده
عکس اوپنهایمر و پاتریس لومومبا
مبل قرمز در حراجی ی الیاس

چارقدهای بته دار آبی رد شدند
آکاردئون و پرچم‌های عزا
ترک‌ها کُردها
عموهایم با عکسشان ته قلیان
مادرم در صف اول نماز جمعه پشتش به من
برادرم عضو بسیج

اول ملخ‌ها می‌آیند بعد شقایق‌ها

Glaucoma

The corn poppies came first,
then the locusts
and after that the unravelling wind.
That was how childhood looked to you
before the dark water, before the thorns,
before the mountain range of a thousand mosques
cast shadow over those wild flowers.

First the poppies went
then Grandmother,
then the royal rooms grew shabby,
the photos of Oppenheimer, Lumumba,
the red furniture – everything went to the second hand shop.

Joyous accordions and flags of mourning,
Turks and Kurds,
little blue patterned headscarves –
all passed by in the street.
'By Appointment to…' the Princes, my father's brothers,
was stamped on every cup and shisha,
my mother, first in line for Friday prayer, kept her back to me,
my brother joined the Bassij.

First the locusts come, then the poppies
no

نه؛ اول شقایق‌ها رفته بودند
و ملخ‌ها ...

گودی چشم از برف پر می‌شد
دره‌های زمستان سفیدِ سفید
بعد تیغ است و آب‌های سیاه

first the poppies went

then the locusts…

The hollow of the eye   fills with snow,

the valleys of winter are white,

then come the thorns and the dark waters……

با گلی سرخ

با گلی سرخ از میان پیراهن‌های سیاه
و پرچم‌های ژنده پیاده‌رو بگذر
راهی دیگر نیست
با گل سرخت
از گوشه چپ کاغذ پایین بیا
از لابلای خطها و سطرها عبور کن
و سمت خاطراتم بپیچ

مرا ملاقات کن
در خانه‌ای زرد و فرسوده
که لولاهای زنگ‌زده دارد
و دریچه‌های پوشیده از پیچک و علف
نجواهای درهم و کشدار غبار اشیاءند

لفاف غمناک سالیان
برگرد ترس‌ها
با گل سرخت بیا بیا
و چنان‌که نبینند
سوی در بهشت اشارت کن

With a Red Flower

Wearing a poppy
leave behind those black clothes,
the flags of mourning,
the tired, disconsolate streets.
This is the only way forward.
Wearing your red flower
climb from between these handwritten lines,
turn from the empty space of this paper
and step into my memories.

Come! Meet me
in that shabby old house,
where now the pipes are rusty,
the shutters lost in ivy and long grass,
where cobwebs and whispers have
settled over everything,
where, after all these years,
sorrow is the only dustsheet.

Come back to me, hide your fears,
wearing your red flower, come back,
but take care that no one sees
you tell me the path you took to Heaven.

نگاتیو یک عکس دسته‌جمعی

در این عکس جوان‌ترم
جوان‌تر از تمام جمله‌های جعلی
و سوم شخص غایب

زیر بلوز و دامن حرف‌هایم برجسته
مثل پروانه‌ای در جلد تابستان
به شگردی از لای انگشت‌ها
شاعرانه از درزهای مخفی بیرون پریدم

قلبم به‌دقت تحت نظر بود
با دو قدم فاصله پشت خودم کمین
برهنه نشسته بودم
در آن سیاهی دنبال صنوبری بی‌رحم
شاید پی ریسمانی سبز می‌گشتم
غزاله حتمن یادت هست؟

در این عکس جوان‌ترم
جوان‌تر از سایه‌ام تنم
و هرچه باید ننویسم
برای جبران زیرپوست دخترم
مادرم را تنگ پوشیدم
چرخیدیم رو به ابرهای نخستین
چرخیدیم تا ریشه‌های باران را بگیرم

Negative of a Group Photograph

I am younger in this photograph,
younger than anything I've ever written,
and I am the third missing person.

Inside me, undercover, my words were taking shape.
Like a moth waking from its cocoon into summer,
peering out from between my fingers,
from my hiding place, as a poet, I stepped out.

Keeping my heart well-hidden,
holding myself back a little
I sat exposed.
In the darkness I searched for that merciless tree
and maybe the trace of a green rope.
For you must remember Ghazaleh?

I am younger in this photograph,
younger than my own shadow.
Anything that I could not write
I disguised, hiding myself in my daughter,
losing myself in my mother.
We sought relief in the first sign of spring rain
but my heart will always ache with the loss of these women.
For you must remember Nazanin?

اما در سینه‌ام هنوز جای هفت زن
همیشه زخمی و خالی‌ست
نازنین حتمن یادت هست؟

آن روزها از جنگ دیوانه‌تر
صدای سکوت می‌آمد
با کلمه‌های ترسیده
زیر پتوی کهنه سربازی
شعر تنها آغوش امن تا مرا بغل بگیرد
زبانش اگر نمی‌گرفت
روی کودکی
لای شکاف‌ها
پشت سین و جیم
به رمز خطی می‌نوشت شکسته‌بسته
بین تابستان و شاخه‌های کبود
فاصله می‌افتاد

بین‌راهی که پیچید دور گلویم
حرفی که در دهانت آتش گرفت
فکر نمی‌کنم مرا یادت باشد؟

در این عکس
از هر طرف سایه‌ها را با قیچی بریدم
خطهایت دوباره ادامه دنیاست
شعر تنها پیرهن عیدی که من بلد بودم
و عشق زیباتر از همیشه
سرهای ما کنار هم نزدیک شانه‌اش

Those days were crazier than any war,
an almost-silence
where words were whispered fearfully
under an old army blanket.
Only poetry could hold us close,
when it wasn't lost for words itself.
Between the shape-shifting letters
peeped a child's face,
the writing all disjointed and hard to decipher.
Between Winter and Summer
the overcast skies pushed us apart.
Between the road that twisted around my neck
and the words that took fire in your mouth,

I don't think that you remember me?

With a pair of scissors,
I trim away all shadows from the image
clothing us afresh for Spring.
Your lines were another new beginning
and poetry the only fresh clothes that I knew,
a love that was more beautiful than ever.

We are strangely young in this picture,
our heads resting against one another,
intimate, affectionate – there I am.

در این عکس عجیب جوان‌تریم
باارادت، آهسته و صمیمی
دوستدار همیشگی‌تان

در نگاتیو لکه‌های سفید و تاریکی
با لبخندی تمام‌قد چفت دیوار
رو به دنیا خبردار ایستاده‌ایم

به یاد غزاله علیزاده و نازنین نظام شهیدی

36

In this stained old black and white negative

with our enormous fixed smiles,

we faced the world, standing tall.

In memory of the poets Ghazaleh Alizadeh and Nazanin Nezam Shahi who both died young and in unfortunate circumstances.

آواره

کفی خاک در مشت می‌برم
در گوشه‌ای از روحم
باران مدام می‌بارد
بر طرح نخل‌های ویران
بر ماه واژگون

آیا هنوز وطن جایی است
روی نقشه جغرافی
با کناره‌های سبز
با رگانِ فیروزه

وقتی باد برده است خانه‌ام
کشتگاهم
اسبم
چراغم
کفش‌هایم را جا گذاشتم زیر تاق شکسته
شویم را به دره‌ای تاریک
پسرانم را سپردم
یکی به دجله
دیگری به فرات

کجاست وطن
جز هاله زخمی به کنج یاد
تا ببری خسته خمیده و خاموش   از پیچاپیچ راه‌ها
نیمی به دل
نیمی به دوش

Homeless

In my fist I take a handful of earth.
In a corner of my soul
lies a landscape of desolate palm trees,
where the rain never stops falling
and the moon hangs upside down.

Is Home still a place
in the atlas
– green borders and turquoise veins?

When the wind has taken my house
my lands
my horse
my light,
when I had to flee barefoot, when I've lost even the roof over my head,
my husband in a dark valley,
my sons entrusted
one to the Tigris,
the other to the Euphrates,

where, then, is Home?
Other than in the corner of my memory
in that ruined halo which – clapped out, collapsing, quiet
from those twisting, turning roads – you carry
half in your heart
half on your back.

زندان

پله‌پله با چشم‌بند تیره‌ات
در ظلمت پایین می‌روی
گودی خواب‌ها
دیواره‌های لیز
وزش بویناک مرگ
هنوز ماسیده کنج لب‌هایت خنده‌های ناتمام
که گردت می‌چرخند ارواح سبزپوش

دیگر در زمین جایی نیست
مگر اتاقی بی دریچه
اینجا بوی کافور می‌دهد
نمی‌دانم در کنام اژدها چرخ می‌زنم
یا پلنگی سیاه دندان می‌ساید بر بازوان و دستانم

ژرف در اعماق تاریکی
آه مادر
انگار بلعیده‌ای مرا و نامی ندارم
همچون جنینی کور میان ریشه‌های پیچان
شست خونینم را می‌مکم
نبض زمین در شقیقه‌های من می‌تپد
سؤال می‌کنند
سؤال می‌کنند
وحشت بند نافم را جویده است
فرومی‌افتم در مغاک بی‌انتها

Prison

One step at a time, blindfolded,
you go down into the dark.
Deep down over the
slippery edge of dreams,
past the sour breath of death,
unfinished laughter caught in your throat
now that green uniforms surround you.

There is nowhere else to go,
only a room with no door,
and the stink of camphor.
Is this a dragon's lair
or in these infinite depths
am I to be torn apart some other way?

> Mother!
> It is as if you have swallowed me whole,
> nameless, a blind foetus
> amongst these twisted roots,
> where I suck my bloody thumb.
> The earth's pulse beats through my temples,
> asking questions
> asking questions.
> Fear eats away at my umbilical cord.
> I fall back into nothingness.

در جهان دیگر صدایی نیست
مگر خش‌خش کاغذها
وزوز حشراتی غریب
روی دست‌ودلم

همه‌جا نگاهمان می‌کردند
در صف‌های بلند
یا درون خلوت رویاها
مانده‌ی شوره‌های اشک بر ناخن
یا آنچه دُرد بسته
بر ته فنجان و جام‌ها
میان خاموشی سبزفام بیدها
دیوی پنهان است
هیولایی گوش خوابانده
درون سیم‌های باریک
آرام بگذرید و سخن نگویید

جهان چنین بی‌رحم بود و نگفتنی
نگفتنی که رد بوسه‌ها می‌ماند
چنان‌که جای تازیانه به پهلو و گرده‌ها
و عشق قامت مرگ بود
خرامان آمد
در پیاله‌ی دستش جرعه‌ای زهرآلود
دروازه‌ها را می‌گشایند حالا
هلهله می‌کنند نقل می‌پاشند
صفی از عروسان
با گونه‌های پریده‌رنگ
با مژه‌های گردآلود

In this world the only sound
is the rustle rustle of paper
and the buzz buzz of insects
on my hand, in my heart.

But everywhere they are watching us,
in the long queues,
in the sanctuary of dreams,
in the tears that fall on my fingertips,
in the dregs at the bottom of cups and glasses,
in the green-shaded silence of the willows
a demon hides.

Quietly, from inside the narrow telephone wires,
something listens in. Say nothing.

The world is merciless, impossible to find words for,
it silences us – but like a welt from a whip
the trace of a kiss will remain.
Love is a match for death.

Terror arrived looking so graceful,
offering its poisoned cup.

Women strolled in through the opening gates
to applause, clap clap clap,   to a confetti of sweets
a row of brides
faces white as a sheet
eyelashes gathering dust.

عروس سیاه‌چالم من
میان ساقه‌های سیاه دل‌تنگی
با گل‌هایی از فلز بر دستانم
مادر! این زمین دنباله‌ی دامن تو بود
سایه‌روشن دوزخ و رؤیا ...
و آن شراب تلخ که نوشیدم
شیر تو بود
من همیشه کودک تو
نوزادی پیر پیچیده در قنداقه‌ی گل‌ولای
انسانی خرد کوچک و خسته

در جستجوی بذر پنهان آتش
شب را پس می‌زنم
و نگاه می‌کنم
به اسکلت‌هایی که گلوله‌ای از سرب
میان سینه‌شان دارند
به یاد می‌آورم
باز ماه برآمده از پشت کاج‌ها
سیرسیرک جوان بی‌خیال می‌خواند
بهارنارنج عطر می‌افشاند
پشت زخم‌ها زندگی گل می‌دهد دوباره
آن گیسوان بریده انگشت‌های شکسته
و پوست پاره‌پاره را بیاورید
بالا خزیده‌اند از روحم
نیلوفرانی درشت با شتکی از خون

I was bride of the prison

amongst the dark leaves of loneliness,

the flowers that I held were handcuffs.

Mother! The earth that I grabbed at was your apron strings,

a bright shadow of hell and nightmare,

and that bitter wine I drank

was your milk.

I have always been your child,

an ancient newborn swaddled in mud,

a tiny tired little person

in search of the hidden spark of a fire.

> I push the night to one side
> and look at the skeletons with
> bullets in their chests.

A memory comes to me,

once again the moon is rising behind the pines,

a nonchalant young cricket chirrups,

the scent of orange blossom floods everything,

and despite my pain, life comes into flower, obstinately, once more.

> Shaved heads   broken fingers,
> torn, flayed skin,
> yet thick waterlilies speckled with blood
> open out in my soul.

من زنده‌ام
در شعرهای ناسروده
در تکه‌های گمشده‌ام در باد

I am alive

in poems yet to be sung,

in fragments of myself, scattered to the wind.

آزادی

حتا، وقتی‌که نیستی
روبروی من نشسته‌ای
چراغ، کنار تو می‌سوزد

پس چگونه آن‌همه بادبان سپید
دستمال کوچکی شد
با نقش مغموم نیلوفری کبود

آونگ ساعت موریانه‌ی زردی شد
و انگشت‌های ما را جَوید
عطر داغ گونه‌های کال تو را

رنگ آن تمشک‌ها
که چیده بودیم؛ سرخ سرخ
و کتاب‌ها را آتش خواند
باد ورق زد

حتی، وقتی‌که نیستی
روبروی ما ایستاده‌ای
چراغ را در ظلمت بالا گرفته‌ای
و ما را به نام می‌خوانی

Freedom

Even when you are no longer here
you sit there, opposite me,
the light burning beside you.

So how did those big white sails
become little paper handkerchiefs,
or change into bruised waterlilies?
Time hatched as a little yellow ant
and nibbled away at my fingers.

Oh, the scent of your tender young blush,
the colour of the raspberries
you picked, red, a searing red
and the books the fire consumed –
are ashes scattered to the wind.

Even when you are no longer here
you stand there, opposite us,
you hold up a light in the darkness,

and you call us by our names.

در گودی زمان

باران‌های پاییزی یکسر باریدند
و آب بالا آمد در گودی روزها
پرندگان و سروها
اسبانی از جنس ماه
و علف‌های رسته از آتش غرق شدند
کلمات چون حباب‌های نقره در ظلمت ترکیدند
و اندود ماه را هیچ ناخنی نخراشید
عشق را آ ب برده است
و روی حافظه حفره‌هایی تهی است
با کناره‌هایی سبز

دیگر چیزی به یاد ندارم
جز خیابانی مه زده
و عبور مکرر زنی با پیکر مشبک
که طناب‌های نامریی
از نرده‌های استخوانی اندوهش گذشته‌اند

نمی‌دانستم از کلمات و سبزینه
از ترانه و رویا
تنها رشته‌ای ناپیدا می‌ماند
تا نگاه داردمان

In the Depths of Time

The autumn rains rained and rained
and water pooled in the space between days.
The birds, the cypress trees,
the moonlit horses
and the crimson leaves, born into heat, all drowned.
In the darkness, words burst like silver bubbles
but the face of the moon had not a mark upon it.
Love had been washed away
and the soul, hoarder of memories, was an emptiness
between green borders.

Now, all that comes to me
is a misty road
and the endless journeying of a woman
whose jagged body
was held back
by invisible ties,
a rope ladder of despair.

I didn't know
that from so many words,
from all that green,
from songs and dreams,

بر این لبه‌ی لیز بارانی
وقتی خم می‌شویم
تا تصویر کبودمان را
میان کبوتران مغروق
و اسبان آبزی نگاه کنیم
و هشت پای ناتوانی
گلوی گریه‌ها را می‌فشارد.

only a thread would remain

to hold us steady

on this ledge, slippery with rain,

where we bend down amongst drowned pigeons

and sea creatures to look,

lassitude, a lump in the throat.

اما

پشت به یکدیگر ایستاده‌ایم
به تماشای تاریکی و جر جر باران
باران می‌ایستد
فصلی دیگر می‌آید
سر می‌چرخانیم
تا بهار را تماشا کنیم
اما یکدیگر را بازنمی‌شناسیم

But

We stand back to back
to contemplate darkness
and the chirping of rain,
when it eases
a new season dawns,
we turn our heads
to contemplate Spring
and find we no longer know one another.

صحنه

بعد یکی آمد
و صحنه را آورد
روی چرخ‌های بزرگ چوبی
اسبی کور با زین و یراق و شرابه‌ها
که از شکمش پایین شدند
نخل‌های اریب و خیس
کوچه‌های باریک و تنگ
عصرهای کمی خاکستری

کشتی‌ها آمدند
با پرچم‌های بلند و یک وجب دریا
ارواح رفتگان، قدیسان
ما که آمدیم غوغا بود
سال‌ها هم را ندیده بودیم
هم را ندیده بودند سال‌ها
یکی از ما دیروز بود؛ آن دیگری فردا
صورتمان را به شیشه چسباندیم
عکس‌ها روی هم افتاد
خندیدیم
شبیه هم بودیم

بعد باد آمد و درون ساعت شد
یکهو زنی رسید

A Panorama

Someone came

and put up a stage,

large wooden wheels,

a blinkered horse, saddled,

its harness and tassels

hanging down round its belly.

Rain-soaked palms, tilting over,

tight narrow streets,

afternoons that were always a little grey.

The boats came

with their tall sails, a drop of the ocean

and spirits of the long-departed, saints.

When we arrived there was pandemonium,

we hadn't seen each other for years,

they hadn't seen each other for years.

One of us was yesterday, the other was tomorrow,

and when we stuck our faces to the glass

our reflections mingled.

We laughed,

we looked so alike.

Then the wind rose and Time shifted again.

با لباس‌خوابی سفید، پابرهنه و کمی گیج
سمت بهشت را پرسید

شلوغ است
از انحنای این جمله‌ها؛ برمی‌گردیم ما
پیچیدیم از پشت پرچم‌ها و عصر
از دور دیدیم؛ صحنه را بردند
خلوت شد

بعد دریا بود
و لباس‌خوابی زیر نور ماه بر یک صندلی
ما برگشتیم
شعله‌ی چراغ را کمتر کنیم

پیازها دارند می‌سوزند

A woman turned up
in a long white negligee, barefoot and a little dazed,
she asked where she might find the way to Heaven.

It was teeming out there.
We turned back from the twist of that cursive,
turned from the tall sails and the afternoon.
From afar we could see that they had taken the stage,
it had grown quiet.

The sea,
a negligee on a chair in moonlight.
We turned back
to lower the heat

the onions were burning.

نامه

سکوت خواب‌های زیادی دید
و به یاد آورد شبح کسی را در آسمان
تو پرنده‌ای شدی با زخمی بزرگ‌تر از سایه‌ات
و به یاد آورد انگشت‌هایت را با آن رد کبود
دو بال بریده کوچک در پاکت
و به یاد آورد
چقدر ما خوب جنگیدم
تا فراموشی مرگ را بغل کند

سکوت مثل درختی ایستاده
هی سبز می‌شود برگ می‌دهد
میوه‌ها فانوس روشنی از خون
طولانی‌تر از کلمه‌هایی که ما را کوتاه برید
و خالی نوشت
در این تهی تیز است چاقوی تو
پر از سیاهی گودال کنده در طول سال‌ها

سکوت ما را ادامه داد
ادا کرد در خواب‌های بد
در این هوای گرفته ابری به دور ما پیچید
تا باور کنی
باران از ابرهای تو همیشه روشن‌تر است.

Letter

In the silence dreams came
and brought to mind   your silhouette against the sky
and you   changed into a bird   carrying hurt bigger than your
   own shadow
and this brought to mind   your cold, stained fingers,
those cut and folded wings placed in an envelope
and that brought to mind
how well we fought
to the bitter end.

Silence, in which you stand like a tree
putting out green, unfolding your leaves,
bountiful; a lantern glimmering with blood-red fruit
so much riper than
the sharp words that cut us short, hollowed us out.
In this emptiness
your knife is still sharp
it has gouged a pit in the passage of years
full of darkness.

Silence, in which we carried on,
making us act out bad dreams,
enfolding us in all those dark clouds,
proffering no handy little mirror for you to look in
and understand
that rain is brighter than anything your clouds could offer.

فانوس‌ها و گهواره‌ها

چون حالت پریشان اقاقی
با خوشه‌های آویخته
چلچراغ سنبله‌های سپید در باد لرزان

در ثانیه‌های مینا رنگ اتاق
سکوت تو: آرامش غریب مرجان‌ها بود
تنهایی من: اندوه تکامل مرواریدی در صدف

گویی آب می‌پوشاند همه زمین
همه شاخه‌های سرگردان و فانوس‌ها
همه گهواره‌ها را

درد عبور عاصی تندباد در تنگی کلام
عشق پروانه‌ای در بند شیشه‌ای
من دیوانه‌وار لحظه‌هایم را تراشیدم
تا راه بگشایم از این دریچه
تا وسعت مکرر آتش
تا صدای غزل‌های عیسی
در کوچه‌های اورشلیم
اینک همه زمان‌ها دورند

موسای کوچک در سبدی نئین
بر نیل می‌رود هنوز
من در تنهایی عتیق خویش
چون ذره‌ای از سیاره‌ای متلاشی
هنوز در راهم

Every Tangled Branch

The locust-tree looked ruffled,
its hanging clusters
like chandeliers of white ringlets trembling in the breeze.

In the azure-tinted moments of that room
your silence was the strange calm of coral,
my loneliness was grief, the way a pearl slowly forms in its shell.

You say that water covers the whole world
every lantern and cradle, every tangled branch.

The ache that followed that tempest cannot be put into words.
A flame-loving moth caught in a glass –
like a madwoman, I trimmed tiny moments
so that I could open up a path to this small door,
walking into the heart of the fire time and again,
to the sound of ghazals
in the streets of Jerusalem.
Those times now seem so far away

Moses in his basket of reeds
still floating down the Nile.
In my antique loneliness,
like a mote of dust from some broken planet,
I am still on my way.

تو همه کودکان و مردان باش
فردای زمین که بازخواهد آمد
از انجماد آب‌های تاریکِ چرخان

You are both man and child to me,
tomorrow will come again for us
out of these cold, dark, swirling waters.

برف

از چین تا ماچین پهنای این ملافه
بر تمام آن برف باریده
چرا نمی‌رسیم؟
جز لنگه گوشواره‌ای
بر این سپیدی ردی نیست
نه درختی هست نه خرگوشی؛ ستاره‌ای
کجاییم؟

گوشواره را انداختی در کشو
ملافه‌ها را در سبد
و تاریکی را تکاندی از ایوان
کنار دست‌هایت کمی مرده بودم

در انتهای شبی که بوی جنگل می‌آمد
اما تمام راه را پوشانده بود
برفی که می‌بارید
می‌بارد
می‌پوشاند هنوز...

Snow

This sheet that stretches from here to the world's end
is covered by all that fallen snow.
Why must we be lost too?
Just a single stray earring
shows midst all this whiteness,
not a tree, not a rabbit, not a star.
Where are we amongst it all?

When you chucked the earring in that drawer
shook out the darkness on the balcony
and threw the sheets into the laundry basket,
at the end of that long night
I died a little.

It was a fresh, wild garden,
but every path was covered
with sheets of snow.
It is falling now, shrouding everything still …

کلمات

خود را پشت کلمات گم می‌کند
تا به دنبالش بگردی
با لحن باد صدایت می‌زند
تا سر بچرخانی
با شعله‌ای علا مت می‌دهد
از بین جمله‌ها سرک می‌کشد
با نقاب
لای عطر سوسن‌ها غیب می‌شود
تا از بیراهه تاریک
دیوارها را دست بسایی و بیایی
تا بعد از پلی لغزان و مارپیچ پلکانی نمور
در قدیمی را دوباره بکوبی
و ناگاه مرا کنار خود پیدا کنی
در هیئت زنی که هیچ شباهتی به او ندارد

Words

She hides herself behind words
so that you have to search for her.
With the song of the wind she calls to you
so that you will turn to her.
She sends up a flare,
she peers up out of sentences
and from beneath a veil
she slips into the scent of a lily,
so that through this wilful obscurity
you'll have to chip away at walls,
cross the slippery, twisty bridge, climb the spiral staircase
come to knock on that old door again
– and look! – find me at your side,
in the shape of a woman who is nothing like her.

آنچه بوده‌ام

همه زن‌ها تمام مردانی که بوده‌ام
خواب‌هایی که رویاهای مرا دیدند
رویاهایتان که من زیستم

اندوهی که مانده بود تا من بگریم
سرودها، بادها و ترانه‌های پنهان
که اینجا وزیدند در هنگام‌های من

تمام زن‌هایی که بوده‌ام
نشانه‌هایی که باد جابجا کرده ست
چشم‌های تو و چهره‌های بی‌شمار
رخساره‌ات و چشم‌های من

تمام پیکرها که بوده‌ای
سنگ‌ها، کبوتران و کاج‌ها
کاج‌ها، سنگ‌ها و کبوترانی که بوده‌ام

تمام برف‌هایی که باریدم
دریاهایی که در تو چرخیدند
راه‌های دیگری و گام‌های من
گام‌های دیگری و راه‌های تو

تمام آوازهایی که خوانده‌ام
با دهان تو چهره تمام زن‌ها
همه مردانی که بوده‌ام

That Which Once I Was

All the different men and women I have been,
the sleep that has seen my dreams,
your dreams that I have lived out,

every sadness that stays with me so that I weep
songs, hidden melodies, zephyrs
that are the music of my life,

every woman I have ever been
blown from place to place by the wind,
your eyes, so many faces,
your face, my eyes,

every shape that I have ever taken
stones, birds, trees,
every tree, bird, stone that I have ever been,

every snowfall,
every ocean that has swilled through you,
every different road that I have walked, my footsteps,
the footsteps of others and each of your roads too,

all the songs that I have sung
through your mouth
into the face of every woman, every man that I have been.

شعر

همیشه هنگامی پیدایش می‌شود
که عقربه‌ها قفل‌اند
و کلمات خواب‌آلود، آن‌قدر دور
که تنها پشت‌شان پیداست
من گیج و برهنه‌ام
خیس از تاریکی، مچاله از سرما
کور از برق سفیدی ی کاغذ
ترحم برانگیزم، هرچند اندکی حیله‌گر
تا مجبور شود تابستان را به دورم بپیچد
اشیایی غریب را به گردم بیاویزد
پرنده‌ای از شعرهای نیما
آیینه‌ای کش رفته از سیلویا پلات
خیابانی که در برف‌ها گم شد
یا چشمان شما، که زیبا بود
اما درست در همین لحظه
ممکن است سرش را بخاراند
نگاهی به آسمان بیندازد
دستش را به شاخه‌های عصر بگیرد و بپرد
و مرا زیر باران‌ها جا بگذارد
کاردستی خیس و مضحکی
که شما آن را خواهید شناخت
اگر روزی از این کتاب رد شوید

72

Poem

In the end it always comes into focus,

that moment when Time shifts

and the drowsy words,

so distant that only

their backs could be glimpsed, turn round.

And though I am confused, weakened,

damp, crumpled from darkness and cold

blinded by the brilliance of a blank sheet,

though – yes, I may arouse pity – I am still a shape-shifter,

and find myself wrapping summer round me,

drawing strange images to me,

a bird from a Nima Youshij poem,

a mirror stolen from Sylvia Plath,

a street that was lost in snow

or your eyes, that were so very remarkable.

Yet just at that moment

maybe the poem will turn its head,

cast a look at the sky,

grab the horns of the afternoon and leap away,

leaving me under the rainclouds

with my ridiculous, hopeless attempts

that you may well recognise

if you happen on this book someday.

Happy Valentine

هفت‌کوه؛ شش دریا و دو آسمان تِبانی کرده‌اند؛ دروغ‌گویند
کی به تو گفت دوستت دارم؟
توی گل‌های شیپوری زار می‌زنم: از تو بیزارم
توی رودخانه‌هایت آهک ریختم   روی ملافه‌ها مرکب
شکل عفریت   کشیدم روی بالش
شاخ دیو روی عکست از تو بترسند ماهی‌ها

به دکمه‌هایم قفل محکمی بود به نوک پستانم طلسم
همه درخت‌های کوچه را اره کردم از لج
همه فایل‌هایت را پاک
اسمت را چپه صدا زدم؛ پیرهنت را دزدیدم

قیر مالیدم به شیشه ماشینت؛ میخ پاشیدم پیچ جاده‌ها
در توالت رویت قفل رفتم سینما؛ بی‌خیال
توی لیوانت سوسک انداختم توی کفشت پونز
بازی را به هم زدم هرروز
مهره‌ها را از نو دوباره چیدم

وسط حرف‌ها یک باغوحش دریایی
پشت جدایی یک فرودگاه صحرایی کشیدم
شب صدای جن شدم توی گوشه‌ات
بمب ساعتی توی رگ و پی‌ات
کراوات میهمانی‌ات را قیچی زدم زیگزاگ
حرف‌ها را گرداندم مثل باد
کارهایت همه بایگانی لای پوشه...

Happy Valentine

They say it was like the collision of seven mountains, six oceans and
    two hemispheres. Well, they lied.
Who told you I love you? I lament to the lilies, *Actually, I hate you!*
I will fill your rivers with limes, flood your sheets with ink,
I'll draw the devil on your pillow and scare the fish with the horns
    and tail I pin on you.
I'll make my nipples irresistible and put padlocks on my blouse.
I will cut down every tree on your street and delete your every file,
I will call your name out backwards, I will steal your shirt,
I'll smear tar on your windscreen, scatter nails at the bend in the
    road,
I'll lock you in the loo and go see a film without a backward glance,
I'll pop a cockroach in your drink and a drawing pin in your shoe,
move all the pieces on the board and ruin every game,
I'll put a desert between us, a whole teeming ocean.
I'll cut your fancy tie into zig zags, I'll slip explosives into your
    nervous system. Each night I'll fill your ears with wailing banshees.
I'll let myself change my mind at the drop of a hat but of your every
    move I'll keep a log.
The very sound of you – Oh god! – it sets my teeth on edge – and,
    even worse,
your gloopy eyes, like bowls of syrup, your stink of saffron and red
    roses,
your heart full of goodluck goldfish, wriggling up against each other!
You know what? If you want to ask me something, I'll tell you

تو بدجور بوی زعفران و گل سرخ می‌دهی
صدایت اه اه شبیه بوق قطار دلم را هُررِی
چشم‌هایت بدتر؛ دو پیاله مسی پر از قند و حلواست
قلبت هزار ماهی قرمز ووِل ووِل توی هم

بعدازاین هرچه بپرسی راست می‌گویم، هرچه بگویی انکار
توی موهایت کوکتل مولوتوف پرت کردم
شبیه آرتور رمبو شوی
انگشتم فرو توی رویاها؛ چک‌چک کند حالت
قورباغه‌ها سوزن شدند زیر لحاف
پرنده‌های شعر اسب پریدند بالای درخت
زن‌ها قوری چینی روی میز اتاق

تمام فلش‌های دنیا خمید سمت چشم‌های تو
خیابان‌ها تا خورد پله‌پله تا کنار پایت
گیج درگیر حفظ شماره طولانی توأم
در استخدام تماشا این گوش و چشم‌های قیقاج
خسته از اضافه‌کاری مدام

از تق‌تق چکش‌ها روی دیوارت ابرها زاییدند
دوری از چنگال‌های تیزم
سازهای نق‌نقو توی دلم رجز خوانند
سماع فیل‌ها روی حلقه آتش
رقص خرس‌های دامن گُلی روی بشکه‌ی باروت
زنجیری ی هندوستان شدم از لهجه‌ی طوطی‌های دیوانه‌ات
کاش قفس بیاورند اژدها ادب شود
اردیبهشت را دوباره تزیین کنند برای بَبر

straight – but if you accuse me of anything, I'll just deny it!

I'll pour a Molotov cocktail into your hair, so you'll look like that
    picture of Rimbaud,

I'll stick my fingers into your dreams, to mess you up altogether,

I'll take over your sleep, you'll think there are frogs needling you
    under those sheets.

I'll turn the sweetest most tender images into ugly ones;

instead of beautiful birds I'll draw horses in the treetops. You know
    those big fat women on Russian dolls? I'll graffiti them all over
    your table!

I'll make you look like a squirrel crossed with a lion and anteater.

Yet I can't just dump you – a tatty, tormenting Tomcat

that can't even find his own way home.

Every arrow points to you. This accordion of streets folds back to you.

But I'm dizzy trying to climb all these summits and towers, trying
    to learn by heart your long number; these ears and eyes of mine
    are worn out with it.

I've banged on your walls so hard the plates are smashed to smithereens.

You may be far away from my sharp barbs but deep inside me it's as
    if elephants sing, spinning hoops of fire and flowery-skirted bears
    dance on barrels.

Your mad jabbering parrots have even got me hooked on an idea of
    India.

If only there was some way to tame this dragon, to put the tiger back
    in its cage. If only it could be Spring again,

before this greedy animal eats up all the white lilies,

تا شیپوری‌های سفید را نخورده این میمون حریص
دنیا را نریخته نپاشیده روی دامنش هیولا

عشق همین گل سرخ است که می‌بندم به سنگ و
پرتاب می‌کنم سمت شیشه‌هات ناغافل
جرنگ و جرینگ و جرنگ
گرمب!

before this monster completely destroys her entire world.

Love is like a red rose that I tie to the stone of myself and aim at your
  window.
Tinkle, tinkle, tinkle.
Crash!

باران‌های اول اردیبهشت

بهتر است مشغول خود باشید
یا شاغل به آنچه معافتان کند
از کار دشوار عاشقی
حرفه‌ای که آدم را وامی‌دارد
تونل‌های بلند و کور
پشت جمله‌های کوتاه حفر کند
با چشم لک‌لک‌ها دنیا را ببیند
زبان مارمولک‌ها را یاد بگیرد
یا مورچه‌ای گیج باشد
که دانه‌های درشت را
از دیوار صاف بالا می‌برد
و از این‌همه مواجبش تنها
بادهای آخر پاییز باشد
و باران‌های اول اردیبهشت

The First Rains of Spring

It is better to bustle away,

to be busy with some work or other

and keep love at bay.

For when it takes hold

we find significance everywhere we look,

the stork's point of view seems persuasive,

we long to learn the language of lizards,

even an ant's dizzying ascent looks meaningful.

And what have we gained from it?

Only the last winds of autumn,

the first rains of spring.

جلسه هیپنوز در مطب دکتر کالیگاری

نه آبی بود عشق نه سرخ نه خاکستری
اتاقی سیاه با مقرنس طلا، تودوزی مخملِ شرابی
دستگیره‌های مذاب و دیواره‌های تاشو رو به دریا
سلام و کلاغ‌های رنگی در یک هوای قدیمی.
سلام و شعله‌ها
و صحنه را دودی ملایم می‌گرداند.

حدود جغرافیایی این خواب از خط چندم مبهم است؟

رود تاریک از اینجا رد می‌شد. سرودِ قایقرانان ولگا. خور خور پاروها در
سینه‌ام. مرد روسی با چکمه‌های گِلی. قطاری مرا به داخائو می‌رفت.
دوچرخه‌ای بی‌صاحب از تماشاخانه برگشت. ساعت چپ‌کوک و مست در
گردنه افتاده بود. کاغذهای برفی و این‌همه کشته در کتاب بی سطر! گل
سرخ؛ زخمی که می‌خزید بالا تا شکل موسیقی

گذشتیم. گذشت
این رابطه تا کجا پیچ می خورد وقتی که راه لغزیده است؟
روی قایق های شناور درخونم حکاکی فیل هاست. روی استخوانم چیزی
بنویس. جوری که نور از تو می چکد و کلمه ها دورمان بازو شدند.
بازیمان گرم بود. لبه دنیا را بگردان روی لبم. پشت الفبا سد و در حاشیه
آبشار است. تا باریکه های سکوت صدا را تا فارسی دل نهنگ پیدا
کند تیمارستان شن از شیب زبان و قاب شیشه ها بیرون بریزد.

Hypnosis Session at Dr Calgari's Surgery

Love was neither blue   nor red   nor grey
A black room with a gold proscenium arch. Wine velvet curtains.
Melty doorknobs and trompe l'oeuil parapets facing the sea.
Words of welcome and brilliantly coloured crows in the antique air.
Words of welcome, flames,
the whole scene swimming in dry ice.

At what point does the setting for this dream become impossible to
    fathom?

A *mighty stream* flows quietly by. The Song of the Volga Boatmen. *Yo!
Heave Ho! Yo! Heave Ho!* Drawing the oars to my chest. A Russian
with his muddy boots. A train to Dachau. A bicycle returns from the
theatre without its owner. An inebriated watch, falls by the wayside,
Time runs backwards. All that blank paper, all this killing, yet no
record of it. Only music murmurs the history of the red rose, of the
wounds.

We passed by. The past passed by.

When did this relationship start twisting and turning? When the
    road grew slippery?

Boats, decorated with little elephants, course through my veins.
Write something on my bones! Light oozes from you. Words put
their arms around us. Our play was passionate. Turn the edge of the
world around and onto my lips. Behind the alphabet there is both
dam and waterfall. Draw out sound to the farthest edge of silence,

گذشتیم. گذشت

بیابان با چه شگردی روایت ورطه‌هاست؟

تاریکیِ هرچه پلک می‌زدم هیچ‌کس. ظلمات وزوز و سطرهای لبریز. وقتی شاخک‌های ماه در آسمان کج شد. و شب با همه تردستی‌اش جواب این شکاف نبود. در نفس‌زنانم مردی با خودش در معاشقه. کم‌کم راه می‌شدم در چاه و لیز می‌آمدم بالا. در اتاقِ عکس‌ها؛ آسانسور فلج در طبقه هفتم. دوزخ زاویه غریب و سردی داشت. چهل طوطیِ خمیده روی کتاب غایب؛ در طلسمات چشم تو یک‌باره سنگ شدند.

گذشتیم. گذشت

بگو آنجا برای رسیدن به‌سوی ما چه خط و نشانه‌ای دارد؟

حالا منظره کجای دیروز است؟. شاید رسیده‌ایم. چشم‌بند سیاه را بازکن. این بوی غول تنها در قوطی کبریت خیس. این اتاق بد قلق. با آینه‌کاری و طاقچه‌های مخفی. کلید را بگیر. بچرخان. این مکعب شاد؛ پهلویش چکه دارد. گوشه‌هایش تَرَک. هرچه دورتر؛ برهنه در خودش راه می‌رود. هرچه دیرتر از کوچه‌های می‌رود؛ رفته است و دوباره تنهاییم. یک مسیر چپ‌اندرقیچی که زیرِآب نشست. اتاقی بی‌سقف. بی ثانیه

و عشق آوار و آهسته
گذشتیم. گذشت

•

until Farsi finds the courage to speak with the heart of a whale. From the sand of a broken hourglass an asylum of language will spill out.

We passed by. The past passed by.

How did the wilderness you spoke of trick you into thinking it dangerous?

The dark. However much I blink, I see no-one. Darkness buzzing, *Before my pen has glean'd my teeming brain.* The moon hangs crooked in the sky and the dark, for all its liquidity, can't cover it up. I hear the sound of a man making love to himself. Little by little I become the path to a slippery well. Pictures fill the room. The lift is stuck on the seventh floor. Hell is a cold and spiky place. Forty parrots are bending over an invisible book and with one look from you, turn to stone.

We passed by. The past passed by.

Tell me, in order for us to find our way, is there a road map?

Now then, what part of the past does this moment belong to? Maybe we have arrived? Undo the blindfold! This place has a bad feeling about it, a hall of mirrors, hidden rooms, the smell of hopelessness – a box of wet matches – a lonesome ghost. Take the key and turn it. This happy box of dripping walls and crevices. This empty room, it turns in on itself. In the end, it shuffles off along the street. It has gone and we are left alone again. No compass. Submerged. A room with no roof. Outside time.

And love quietly falls apart.

We passed by. The past passed us by.

همه‌جا

در انتظار توأم در بلگراد
در مسکو   منتظرت بودم
چشم‌به‌راه تو هستم در بغداد
در دنج‌های خلوت برفی
کافه‌های بنجل؛ عرق فروشی؛ پس‌کوچه‌ها
اتاق ۳۶۷ تختی در تمام هتل‌ها
در کنج ِ تاریک خیابان و جرجر باران
روزنامه‌هایی که   خیس ِ و مچاله...
از اخبار جنگ ؛ آگهی روسپی‌خانه؛ اعلان فروش گربه‌ها

در سونات ِ شکسپیر
سطر دهم از شعر آخر آنا آخماتووا
هر رمان پوسیده‌ی فراموش در کهنه فروشی
هر گلبرگ خشکیده‌ای در لای کتاب
در ترانه لورکا جایی که سروها خم می‌شوند
جرعه‌ای از ته هر بطری قلپی از تمام لیوان‌ها
منتظرت هستم

اسمت آلکس است اگر   گابریل یا حداد
پاییز است روز تولدت   تابستان یا خرداد
با قطارهایی که آمدند

Everywhere

I am waiting for you,
in Belgrade.
In Moscow I look out for you,
in Baghdad my eyes scour the streets for you,
in desolate places, cosy corners, in snowstorms,
in dingy cafes, at the off-licence, in side streets,
in Room 367 and in every other hotel room.

At the dark end of the street, in the pitter-patter of rain,
in torn, wet newspapers
among the stories of war, prostitution and small ads for kittens,
in the sonnets of Shakespeare,
or the tenth line of Akhmatova's final poem
in every tatty forgotten novel at the flea market,
in every flower petal pressed between the pages of a book,
in Lorca's songs, where the cypress trees bend low,
when I drink the dregs of every bottle, when I gulp down every glass
   I am waiting for you.

Whether your name is Alex or Gabriel or Hedad,
in autumn, on the day of your birthday or in summer,
in the rattle of a train, in the sound of the ship's whistle as it leaves,

کشتی‌هایی که بوق زدند وقت فرار
هر اتوبوس لکنته‌ی آبی‌رنگ
کنار دکه فروش بلیت ؛ روی سکو؛ زیر تمام تابلوها
منتظرت هستم

گوری که در آن دفنم کردند و یادت رفت
با لباس عروسی زیر نور ماه در نقاشی شاگال
برهنه لمیده روی کاناپه‌ی مخمل ِ شیری‌رنگ
با همین پیش‌بند آشپزخانه چرب پر از لکه‌ها
چشم‌انتظار توأم

داری با شتاب می‌آیی یا برمی‌گردی بی‌حوصله
با همین زیرپوش ؛ کفن و کلاهی که دوستش نداری
با لاله‌های زرد ؛ کتاب کاما سوترا و شیشه شراب
به همان اسم و قرار و حقه‌هایی که عاشقش بودی

هر جا گم شوی از هر طرف بپیچی
در تمام ایستگاه‌های زمین

منتظرت هستم

on every tired old blue bus,

by the ticket seller's booth, sitting on the sofa, in the surface of every

  painting,

      I am waiting for you.

Here I am in the grave in which they buried me, the one you forgot,

in my wedding dress, in the moonlight of a Chagall painting,

naked, stretched out on a milky-coloured velvet sofa,

my apron, greasy and covered in stains,

      I am longing to see you.

Are you rushing back to me, or are you dragging your feet?

In just a camisole, in a shroud or in a hat that you don't like,

armed with yellow tulips, the karma sutra and a bottle of wine,

with all the same old tricks that you loved so,

wherever you lose yourself, whichever way you turn,

in every station on this earth,

      I am waiting for you.

اینجا حومه‌های کلاغ است

باران‌ها از همین سمت رفته بودند
با کیف و با کلاغ
پرسش‌ها کودک می‌نوشت
چرا مگر آیا اگر
دست که می‌انداختند در گردنم دیوانه‌های سپیدار
روی دوچرخه عباس را می‌دیدم

لطفا پرچم نیاویزید بر نرده‌ها سیاه
این صحنه زیباست
تنهایی را زخم‌ها می‌تند
و راه می‌کشد
در جاده‌هایی که دورند تا دیگر
نه مثل اینجا که باروی کهنه‌ای است غروبش
آسمان را زشت می‌بافد چرا
و خیابان‌هایش تا هرگز نمی‌رسند

می‌خواهم کوچک برگردم
کوچه‌ها را مشت مشت خالی از برف
تخته‌سیاه را بسوزانم آیا
تا دور می‌زنم خودم را
با انگشت‌های خاکی
بر زانوانت عاشق‌ترم

Crow's Final Frontier

The rains headed off over there
where the old poplar trees threw their wild shadows across me,
a child, with my school bag, midst the crows,
my friend Abbas on his bicycle.
I asked these questions –
Why? Why? When? Where? How? How?

Please don't put out those black flags of mourning,
they'd spoil this lovely scene.
Pain only brings loneliness
and starts us
on roads that take us a long way from all we've known,
like here where sunset fades the walls, makes the sky ugly
and the roads lead nowhere.
Why? Why?

I want to be a child again,
to clear the streets of snow, handful by handful,
to turn away from the blackboard – *When?*
to dust myself down with chalky fingers.
I was happier balancing on top of your knobbly knees,
to reach the apples at the top of the tree

از شانه هایت بالاترم تا چیدن های سیب
اینجا زنی ایستاده‌ام مگر
مارها دربازی نقشی نداده‌اند
به موهای تیفوسی‌اش

تا پله را بیاورند
بر لبه‌ام ایستاده‌ام
از سمتی که باران‌ها می‌رفتند
و عباس‌ها از خیابان رد نمی‌شوند اگر
شماره برهوت را بگیر

اینجا حومه‌های کلاغ است
لطفا پس از صدای قارقار پیام بگذارید

happier than I am, standing here now, a woman – *Where?*

Hair shorn,

sliding back down a snake,

until someone brings a ladder,

I am teetering on the very edge,

facing the direction those rainclouds took,

with no old friends like Abbas passing along this street – *How? How?*

Dial the number for No Man's Land

'This is the final frontier of crow territory,

Please leave a message after the caw.'

بهار

ای باد آیا گذشتی
از کوچه‌های حلبچه؛ خرمشهر و کربلا
آنجا چگونه شکفته شاخه‌های نخل
در بغداد از کودکان بسیاری نماندند
تا بپوشند اولین کفش عمر خود
و گام بردارند با مادر در شارع الحمید
آب‌نبات‌چوبی بخواهند
یا عروسکی کوکی

در آبادان نه بر گهواره کودکی‌ست
نه باغچه‌ای سبز است
نه ایوان خانه از نسترن چراغان
آن پسرک سبزه روی بندر اگر بود
حالا مردی بود بلندبالا و مشکین موی
می‌توانست عاشق باشد
کتاب بخواند
خانه بسازد
و باد بکوبد در خانه او را

اما بانوی ما بهار
هرسال به لحظه موعود دوباره می‌آید
تا عبور کند از هزار دروازه شفاف
اسب‌های شعله‌ور ابر به دنبالش

Spring

Ah, wind, did you breeze past
the streets of Halabja, Khorramshahr and Karbala?
Have the date palms blossomed there yet?

In Baghdad many children didn't last long enough
to wear their first pair of shoes
and toddle with their mothers down Al Hamid road,
to long for lollipops
or clockwork dolls.

In Abadan, there are no babies in the cradles,
no green gardens,
no balconies lit up with eglantine.
If that little olive-skinned boy from the port were here
he would be a man by now, tall with jet-black hair,
he might have fallen in love,
read books,
built a house,
the wind might have tapped at his door,

but, our lady, the Spring,
each year, at the promised hour, she returns,
to slip through a thousand glassy gates,
the galloping clouds aflame at her heels,

او همیشه می‌آید
گاه با گوری در سینه‌اش
دامنی سوخته در جنگ
صورتی آغشته به گل
به باروت و بوی نفت
آمده است که باز ببافد
با نخ‌های نیلگون
که شکافته از جامه تنگ سال پیش
تصویر یک پرنده را
پشت هر دریچه و ایوان

رنج را نگینی سبز جای چشمانش
زخم را طرحی جای منقارش
تا همیشه سرخ بخواند

she always comes back

sometimes with death at her breast,

skirts singed by war,

face stained with mud,

gunpowder, the stink of petroleum,

she returns to use again

all that she unpicked from last year,

sewing, in every nook and cranny, in cerulean thread,

the image of a bird –

pain, like a green stone, in place of its eyes

and a wound where its beak should be,

so it can sing out   its scarlet song.

زمستان که بیاید

زمستان بیاید
شکل خودت در آینه پیدا می‌شوی
کتاب‌ها دورت آتش گرفته‌اند
یاسمن در خواب‌هایم آهو می‌دود
سر به کوه می‌زند
کوه به‌سادگی در سینه‌ام جا می‌شود
دیدی ترسی نداشت قواره‌ی سنگ‌ها
از افتادن بالا که می‌رویم
دریا اهلی‌تر می‌آید
قلاده‌اش را گرفته‌ام

پس مرا با کلمات نزن
شکنجه نده
تنت را به صخره‌ها نکش
تا شکل پلک‌های خونی بمیریم

زمستان کوچه‌ای صاف
انتهای همین خیابان است اگر بپیچی
سال‌ها همین اسب سیاه رم کرده
با انگشت که بشمری

زمستان که بیاید
از هر دو سو رفته‌ایم
یکی مرا گم می‌کند

When Winter Comes

When winter comes
I will look in the mirror and know myself again.
On fire with ideas, my books were burning.
My daughter came to me in dreams, a deer running,
a deer that had me flee to the mountains.
Well, I can hug those mountains,
see how they nestle in my arms?

There was nothing to be afraid of after all.
Scale is just a matter of perspective,
even when we fall, we rise up again,
the sea looks calmer,
the fluffy white dog is back on its lead.

So don't berate me,
don't blame me,
don't beat me up about it,
don't make me weep blood.
Count the passing years on your fingers,
they are galloping by like a wild, dark horse
and the only thing at the end of that path is winter.

When winter comes
we can follow one of two paths,
we can get lost

با آن یکی پیدا می‌شوم

اما باید نمی‌ترسیدی و می‌گفتی
چرا به سینه‌ات چاقو فروکرده‌ای
تا آدم‌ها در آینه از تو فراری شوند

or we can find ourselves again.

I shouldn't have been scared,

I should have said, *why torture yourself?*,

so that those shadows melt away, leaving just me in the mirror again.

ماه

هر گوشه زمین باشم
سقف همیشگی تویی
ماه
ای آه مشترک
چرخ جامانده‌ای از گردونه‌ای که برد
رؤیاهای ما را
با کولیان رنگین فصل‌ها
ما مانده‌ایم
و شور باغ‌های نچیده که دود شدند
در پشت پلک‌های تمنا...
ما مانده‌ایم و تو
تو سیب اشتیاق بر رف ظلمت
ما دستانی از فلز
با طرح و قواره خواهش
در کهکشان وقت

Moon

wherever I am in the world

            the roof is always made of you

moon

        we sigh in unison

  a wheel that was left behind

           from our circadian dreams

  a kaleidoscope of gypsies   who travel through the seasons,

           we remain,

and all that fuss over the unkempt garden went up in smoke

       behind a vision   of longing,

we remain   and you

you   the very apple of desire   hang against a roof of darkness.

     we   our hands stilled   we

     are silent shadows   in the Milky Way

قایقی که مرا آورد

پشت چهره‌ای که چشم‌های تو را داشت
اسم‌های قدیمی غیب می‌شود
خون عکسی مچاله دارد
و باد پرنده‌ای مسی است
انگار بیابان مرا از روی ژاکتم پوشیده باشد

برهنه نیستم
گاهی کلمات در سرفه‌هایم
و ماه کف‌آلود در لیوان گم می‌شود
این سفر همیشه دور زبانم چرخید
و رگ‌هایم از مرگ چیزی پنهان نکرد
برای کشیدن قدم‌هایی به خط ثلث
تابستان مرا اقرار کرده بود
این کرک سبز دور انگشت‌های یخ‌زده

موج به طرز زیبایی شبیه عشق
می‌آمد و پس می‌نشست

دلم برای قایقی که مرا آورد
گاهی تنگ می‌شود
و اینجا شاهدم برابر پلک‌های زمستان
همین آسمان کهنه است
و چمدانی که نیم‌رخ آبیِ مرا پنهان می‌کند.

The Boat that Brought Me

Behind these eyes that look like mine
old names are fading away,
the past lies crumpled in my clenched fist –
a coppery bird in coppery wind,
this vast place has covered me from head to toe.

I am not stripped of word and thought
but sometimes what I want to say gets lost
like a moon smudged with cloud, or when I splutter on a drink.
My tongue trips up when I speak of that journey
though the blood in my veins felt the truth of death.
As I traced my footsteps through the tracery of my old language
Summer whispered to me
my frozen fingers began to put out shoots
and I began to love the cold ebb and flow of tides.

Sometimes I miss
the boat that brought me here,
now that I am witness to the icy eyes of a Swedish winter
under these tired old clouds,
while that suitcase still holds a patch of the sky-blue me.

ناگاه

چنان گرم گفتگو بودیم
که تاریکی فرود آمد
و ما را پوشاند
با بال‌های بزرگ نمناکش
چراغی نبود
بر لبه عصر
هاج و واج ایستادیم
کودکانی خمیده و دیر سال
کنار گودی دقایق
به تماشای قایقی کاغذی
که در آب فرومی‌شد.

A Glimpse

So caught up in our conversation

that darkness fell

and covered us

with large damp wings

and not a single light showed

in that blue hour

where we stood

grown-up children

held for a moment, astonished,

watching a paper boat

as the water swallowed it.

قطب‌نما

شهر ساکت و سپید دورت حلقه بست
نفس نداشت الفبا در تنگی هوا
نشد بخوانم برف
فارسی نشد ببارد
و عشق صحرا شود

گفتم به سایه‌ای که نوشتم
دل ببندم به سروهای ناپیدا نشد
تلخ روی زبانم؛ با هر جرعه‌ای زدم
جاده طناب بی‌مصرف به دور پاها
از این حروف راه روشن نشد

ساعت همیشه غروب
سوز هوا شبیه دی‌ماه
کلاغ بیگانه‌ای روی سطر تنها نشستم
غارم خط آخر زمستان
شیب‌ها یخ
جمله‌ها زیر صفر همه
برف روی منقار
همه‌جا برف
در صدایم می‌بارید
سرد و شیری آهسته

آینه را بستم
صمیمی از ته دل نگاه کردم حتا نشد

Compass

The city, quiet with bright ice, held me captive,

language was breathless in its tight air.

I could not sing snow.

Oh for it to rain Farsi!

My mouth was full of longing,

love had dried up.

I told these shadows of my writing –

I can't just lean on memories of cypress trees,

the road that led here has tied my hands,

the path ahead is all muffled up.

It always feels like evening,

there's a December chill in the air,

a stranger-crow I've settled on a telegraph wire,

my caw the last line of winter,

the hill icy,

writing frozen,

snow on the beak,

snow everywhere,

and snow fell quietly into my voice

cold, milky white.

برگشتم با هرچه رنگ

با دست و تمام بال‌ها

روی هر صفحه سفید

به لهجه خودی

برف را عاشقانه فارسی نوشتم

I stopped thinking about myself,

I looked deep into my heart for understanding – but no –

I tried again with every shade I could think of,

with every trick I knew

and then on each white page,

in a voice I recognised,

lovingly, I wrote the snow in Farsi.

از نو

کنار دریا روبروی کوه زیر همین آسمان
زمین را از نو دوباره تا کردم
ماه در چمدانم بود
باران را بلند روی دست گرفتم

اسمم نه مهاجر است اینجا نه تبعیدی
به لهجه محلی دنیا همان‌که خاک مادرم قسم خورد
نشانی‌ام آب است
شعر حالا تنها سفر می‌کند
در جاده‌هایی گیج مثل یک سؤالِ طولانی
که رازشان رد چند بریدگی است
عزیزی که اقیانوس و دره‌ها را به نامش طی کردم
ستاره و صحرا
روی مسیرِ کودکی روشن می‌تابید
باد دزدیده بود جلدم را
در جمله‌ها سنگ زوزه می‌کشید

فقط مسافری که شعر می‌نویسد
نه ان قدر ساده
بسته‌ای کوچک
با روبان رنگی و مهر خاورمیانه
سطری برای عنوان اخبار امشب
تحقیقی برای حد مرگ

I Unfolded the Earth

By the sea   in front of the mountain   under this very sky
I unfolded the earth anew again,
the moon was in my suitcase,
I held the rain up high in my hand.

My name here is neither immigrant, nor exile,
in the true accent of the earth
the one I swore loyalty to, on the grave of my mother,
my emblem is water.
Poetry now travels on alone
dizzy on its path, like the longest of questions,
its secret is a few old scars......
a beloved, in the name of whom I travel the universe, stars,
valleys and deserts,
it shone brightly on my childhood path.

The wind stole my cover
in my sentences, stones howled.

Am I just a traveller who writes poetry?
Not that simple.
A small package
tied with bright ribbons and a stamp from the Middle East,
a detail in tonight's news headlines,
a report on the number of dead

به شکل یک پرچم صورتک سایه

کنار دریا روبروی کوه زیر همین آسمان
پشت درِ بسته
گربه‌ی سفید خانم اسونسون را به سینه چسباندم
کلاغ و سرو و هرچه ساعت
از شدت سکوت از آغوش من پرید
عشق دستش را به جای دوری گرفته بود، نیفتد

من وسواس خوب بودن گرفته‌ام اینجا
مرض اجرای دقیق قانون
شعر اما خودسر و پابرهنه
آس و پاس و بی کجا ...
در حروفش تگرگ و شیشه در جنگند
تلفظ رودخانه در زبان او عمیق و آبی
تنها نه گفتن معنای عاشقانه‌ای دارد

حالا دیوانگی از امضای شما فوری‌تر
خوابی که دیده‌اید به‌شرطِ چرا
یا به‌رسمِ آیا
مرزهای مرا دیگر اهلی نمی‌کند

کنار دریا روبروی کوه زیر همین آسمان
دهانی که قفل بود آهسته بوسیدم
خدانگهدار
برگشتم از بهشتی که "دوستت دارم" بلد نبود
راهی که دیگر تو را نمی‌رفت
محکم مرا زمین کوبید

in the shape of a flag, a small face, a shadow.

By the sea   in front of the mountain   under this very sky
behind a closed door
I have clasped Mrs Sweden's white cat in my arms
but now and then crow and cypress tree
leap from within, from my deep silence,
and love
holds on steadily to something very distant, so that it will not fall apart.

I have become obsessed with behaving well here,
a kind of illness of never putting a foot wrong,
but poetry is headstrong, walks barefoot,
cannot be directed, has no true home,
within its letters, inner and outer worlds are at war,
in its language the river speaks deep and blue
only the word 'no' has a loving meaning.

The conditions, the whys and the wherefores,
a kind of madness with the ease of a signature,
it was a dream I had. New borders will not make me feel at home.

By the sea   in front of the mountain   under this very sky
I slowly kissed goodbye to the mouth that was shut fast
May God be with you
I returned from a paradise that didn't understand 'I love you'
a road that couldn't reach you –
it knocked me flat.

برگشتم
این شعر لخت این آسمان زخمی را بغل کنم
برای صبحی وحشی و درختی پا به راه
شهر دیگری بزایم
روبروی کوه کنار دریا زیر همین آسمان

I returned

and taking this naked poem, that bruised sky into my arms

uprooting myself, I set out on this wild morning

to give birth again to a new city

by the sea   in front of the mountain   under this very sky.

About the Authors

AZITA GHAHREMAN was born in Mashhad in 1962. One of Iran's leading poets, she has lived in Sweden since 2006. She has published five collections of poetry: *Eve's Songs* (1991), *Sculptures of Autumn* (1995), *Forgetfulness is a Simple Ritual* (2002), *The Suburb of Crows* (2008), (a collection reflecting on her exile in Sweden that was published in both Swedish and Farsi), and *Under Hypnosis in Dr Caligari's Cabinet* (2012). Her poems have been translated into German, Dutch, Arabic, Chinese, Swedish, French, Russian, Ukrainian, Turkish, Danish and English. She is a member of the South Sweden Writers' Union.

MAURA DOOLEY has published several collections of poetry, most recently *The Silvering* (2016) which was selected as a Poetry Book Society Recommendation. Her other works include *Life Under Water* (2008) and *Sound Barrier: Poems 1982–2002* (2002) and she has edited anthologies of verse and essays, amongst them *The Honey Gatherers: Love Poems* (2003) and *How Novelists Work* (2000). She has worked with new writers all her working life for, amongst others, the Arvon Foundation, Performing Arts Labs, the South Bank Centre, Jim Henson Film and currently for Goldsmiths College, University of London. She has twice been shortlisted for the T S Eliot Prize and is a Fellow of the Royal Society of Literature. She received a Cholmondeley Award from the Society of Authors in 2016.

ELHUM SHAKERIFAR studied Persian Literature at Oxford University, where she spent 4 years studying everything from Nizami to Forugh Farrokhzad. She is a BAFTA-nominated producer and curator of film, and the 2017 recipient of the Women in Film & Television Award for her documentary work.

Also from the Poetry Translation Centre and Bloodaxe Books

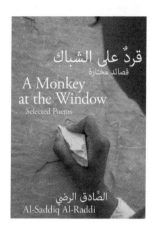

A Monkey at the Window

by Al-Saddiq Al-Raddi

Translated by Sarah Maguire & Mark Ford

Al-Saddiq Al-Raddi is one of the leading African poets writing in Arabic today. Famous in his native Sudan, the vivid imagery of his searing, lyric poems create the world afresh in their yearning for transcendence.

In 2005 Al-Raddi's poems were first translated into English by the Poetry Translation Centre for their first World Poets' Tour. In 2015 his book *He Tells Tales of Meroe: Poems for the Petrie Museum* was shortlisted for the Poetry Society's prestigious Ted Hughes Award.

A Monkey at the Window is Al-Raddi's first full-length collection in English. The book includes a translator's introduction by Sabry Hafez, illuminating the importance of Al-Raddi's work within the Sudanese poetry tradition. A second essay, 'The Promise of Poetry' by Sarah Maguire, the founder of the PTC, relates Al-Raddi's life as a journalist and stadium-filling poet superstar in Sudan under Omar al-Bashir's regime.

poetry
translation
centre

BLOODAXE BOOKS

Also from the Poetry Translation Centre and Bloodaxe Books

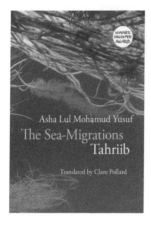

The Sea-Migrations

by Asha Lul Mohamud Yusuf

Translated by Clare Pollard

Although Asha Lul Mohamud Yusuf has lived in exile in the UK for 20 years, she is fast emerging as one of the most outstanding Somali poets, as well as a powerful woman poet in a literary tradition still largely dominated by men. She is a master of the major Somali poetic forms, including the prestigious *gabay*, by which she presents compelling arguments with astonishing feats of alliteration.

The poems in this collection are brought to life in English by award-winning Bloodaxe poet Clare Pollard, in collaboration with Said Jama Hussein and Maxamed Xasan 'Alto'.

'Sometimes a book reminds us of poetry's real electric force in the world. Yusuf is a brilliant young Somali poet, living in exile in London, who takes "history's point / to ink a beautiful literature"... Translated into lapel-grabbing alliterative verse by Clare Pollard, these piercingly direct poems throw open a window onto a war-torn country and its wretchedly displaced people.'

The Sunday Times

poetry translation centre

BLOODAXE BOOKS

Also from the Poetry Translation Centre and Bloodaxe Books

My Voice

A Decade of Poems from the Poetry Translation Centre

Edited by
Sarah Maguire

In this gloriously diverse, revelatory selection of translations from the Poetry Translation Centre's first decade you will find 111 brilliant poems translated from 23 different languages (ranging from Arabic to Zapotec: all the original scripts are included) by 45 of the world's leading poets. Arranged on a journey from exile to ecstasy, these powerful poems have been co-translated by some of the UK's best-loved poets including Jo Shapcott, Sean O'Brien, Lavinia Greenlaw, W N Herbert, Mimi Khalvati and Nick Laird.

> 'This groundbreaking anthology extends the territory of English poetry through a series of generous translations that make welcome the magnificent poetic traditions of many communities now settled here.'
>
> Carol Ann Duffy

> 'Essential reading for anyone writing poetry in the UK today.'
>
> Chrissy Williams, *Poetry London*

poetry
translation
centre

BLODAXE BOOKS